Regarding My Father

Regarding my Father

Poems

Martin Tilling

Grosvenor House
Publishing Limited

The right of Martin Tilling to be identified as the author of this
work has been asserted in accordance with Section 78
of the Copyright, Designs and Patents Act 1988

The book cover photograph is copyright to Shaun Wilkinson
The book cover is copyright to Martin Tilling

This book is published by
Grosvenor House Publishing Ltd
Link House
140 The Broadway, Tolworth, Surrey, KT6 7HT.
www.grosvenorhousepublishing.co.uk

This book is a work of fiction. Any resemblance to
people or events, past or present, is purely coincidental.

A CIP record for this book
is available from the British Library

ISBN 978-1-78623-615-9

To my father and mother, Harold and Sheila Tilling,
and my brother David Tilling.

Thanks for the love and support of David Watt, the rock in my life

Also, thanks to all of my incredibly important extended
family of friends

POEMS

PART III

PART IV

PART I

TO START REGARDING MY FATHER

Beginning with thoughts of their togetherness
And my imagined tales and truths

They now occupy my bedside
The photos I didn't know existed
Or did I?
Perhaps through an uncertain childhood memory
of a glimpse of some of them now and then,
The only word to describe them is gorgeous
Glorious gorgeous images of my mother and father
Bound together by their love and their country church's blessing
Never to be known by us, that large sibling family were all there
Circling and rejoicing

When father left Alan and their ships
We were soon born
And then followed by my bed the next picture of us in their arms
Skin on skin, gentle oneness
Homemade mother's clothes to mirror
each other's beauty and glory
Soon to be mounted in matt silver above our heads

Pregnant parents
Mother was oh so fearful of our labour
But joyous of our coming
She always was to repeat her pain to us
Of course, we knew not its meaning

So, do I remember swirling inside her with him?
At all? Or just as she gently tried to move
up and down the hills of Dove Dale,
On their first visit several months down
Later, on a childhood day, they were to take us back to see that place

And feel we did, or at least I did
So moved was I, thinking of her as I fell down
from reaching up to a tree on a steep slope
Alongside the blue and green bubbling brook,
She remembered and told me that day,
Of her fear as she tried to climb that very hill
Not too many years before, full of us
All day I couldn't get from my mind the feeling
of being her or me or both

No twin until that early autumn birth
I talk of her and us
But in those months, she was me
Me, her daughter to be
Hilary was to be my name
No sibling in her womb with me
Not until the midwife, in her sick last months,
issued her belief that there were to be two
But no other medics thought aught
Till that day in October, month early,
When I was pulled and pulled
Then after David slid out alongside me
We knew, she did not
If only she could have had a sense that we knew more,
however young we were
Of course, we did know
We were in her and of her

That childhood secret of my sick mother
Kept her in for a month before we came
But what is a sickness?
What you endured or how it led to disembowelment by others?
Scared and angry to have to see you shaking, falling, feinting,
maybe even dying
Better to mock than muck in and be with you
Would your desperate love for us risk being lost
by us behaving like them?

"Have faith in your boys", we should have known to say
"We will be with you and give you ourselves", we would have said
We never knew of your illness till you had gone
And I wonder till this day
How your mother, my grandmother,
Was with you about your life-threatening fits

Family adoration at having two, and both boys
When we two came, there was adoration from all
Such jealous surprise, translated to worship
Beside me are more photos of them smiling
and adoring you with us in your arms
The grand family all together
Then slowly, one by one, they were all let go of in our childhood
To utterly focus on us or to unknowingly punish them and us all?

The Lord was to accept and bathe us
Christening in our holy place, preparing us
for a child's Sunday life of choir singing, like Harold's choir and organ
    pumping,
both morning and evening
Just like him, we radiated our identity into the choir chapel's air
Feeling the warmth of its spirituality even though we were uncertain
at that time of the religious meaning
Magnificat and Nunc Dimittis, mid-way in the evensong
Gave me my most reflective joy of that church time

So, life came and went
His and ours
Here now I sit with
my thoughts
A few months down the path

LAST TIME

(1)

Thinking of it
That which made me
Elated and sad
How could that be

(2)

Surprise October warmth
Beckons me to the dunes
Gale like winds
No cooling shivers
Amazing desert heat
Undertow too great
For all to partake

(3)

Tiptoe down the beach
Between each giant wave
Brief calm pulls me down
Enveloped in just warm
Lightly cooling tingles
Floating unconsciously
Unbounded sensory-ness

(4)

When will this next be?
Will it ever come again
Or is this the last time?

(5)

Last autumn swim
Last apple's crunch
Last Edward's lunch
Last mother's touch
Last night with you

(6)

As life lingers
Time shortens
How many last time
experiences
will I remember

HAROLD AND ALAN

(1)
Boys to men
13 years in hand
Up and down
Down beyond
End of the world

(2)
Artic to Antarctic
Tropical traverse
No Rio ride
Carnival reverse
Slide along Sugar Loaf
Surge to South Georgia
Queen to be
Kept them beached up
Whaling akimbo
South of the Weddell Sea

(3)
Meat man assigned
Favoured over fought
The best joints
To his non-favourites naught
But a small cup of grog
If they gave him the nod

(4)
No west coast coast
Three year delay
Then Hong Kong we're coming
Up and away
Again

(5)
Remembering Eden
No live action
War in a canal
Blocked at each end
Egypt won Suez
Still, we both got our medals

(6)
When not on leave
We often passed Gibraltar
En route to Cyprus via Malta
Valetta our favourite
When could we return,
with our wives?
Thirty years later
When we were on our own
   down turn

(7)
They stayed together
Friends – more than that
His wife and girls
Only ones to come and stay
Till Alan started to shake.
But just a few years on
And they were all at his sad wake

(8)
Never more on ship
Or Chatham, Lympstone or Deal
But in the air over the sea
You could find their camaraderie
Shimmering in the sunset
on the ocean's western waves

MAKE YOURSELF SLEEP

Make yourself sleep
Take your eyes and close them
Press the eyeballs hard upwards
So, the light gets pushed back lighter
And orange circles envelop lower down
Then open the eyes in lighter darkness
And see the wall's image come closer and
Larger than reality
Glance up and down following the white dot
Blurring today's reality
And bringing tomorrow's awakening
Through peaceful sleep
Now soothingly gained

THE SPIRAL CARPET

As a young child
I had no questioning conscience
I wandered aimlessly regularly
Often captured in a timeless boundless place

Below the stairs
Beyond the hall
Unable or un-wanting to return or leave
And rushing a few steps from the exit door
I walked on the spiral carpet

Steps leading ever inward, ever smaller
To an infinite un-reachable finishing point
Where I spun on the central woollen thread
Was it red or green or perhaps golden?
Was it a five toothed dragon?
Or the mouth of a baleen whale?
Or my mother's fearless smile?

As I waited for spontaneity to bounce me back
on the outward journey of turning uncertainty
Counting now – which random number would come into sight?
Telling my feet how many more inward and outward
Spiralling stepped trance dances
were needed to permit my admission back into reality

BLACKBERRY BATHING

Mother called us
A few days before
To ready us for a day of magical hours
Her face showed us how joyful the day to come would be
We think we knew about this from the past
Before our memories were rememberable

Bags and baskets, containers of any kind
Were miraculously re-found.
And as I close my eyes now
I can still see my mother's face
Shining blue eyes, smiling lips and clearly tingling skin
Responding to the call of her homeland for the enchantment to come

Now we four arrive on the gated lane
Its own adventurous joys supressed for this day
Having climbed over and through the spiky hedgerow
In the gorgeous burning August sun
Tricky clay clumped field clambered through

We pause momentarily to savour and then start our annual
    blackberry bathe
In the deep country's ever deeper
dark purple, bursting, luminous, deep inner-scented, flooding
    radiance
Wall after wall of nature's gifted fruity vision
Reaching, touching, smothering, gathering
filling our carried containers to bring this bountiful harvest home

But dazed in our bottomless intoxication
Fear suddenly breaks through the berry dam
Evil coloured wasping bees and buzzing wasps
Attack our fragrant mure sprayed skin
Pushing us abruptly away from the forest edge
And then we scream as we are stabbed by

The fruitful creeper's thorny arms
One by one we fall down
Only to be poisoned by the underworld's green stingers
Can we survive, will we be able to re-reach the bathing wall?

Mother calls, father pulls us up
Thankfully no loss of those fruitful fillers
We stretch out for two more hours of submerging
As berries roll and re-coat our skin, from finger tips to
	chests and into the bags
Dark ruby glistening bliss

As the sun begins to turn a redder orange to mirror the berries
We sense the day is closing
This year's berry bathing is coming to an end

Mother and father take the oh so heavy pounds
of fruit back across the undulated tripping field
To the gated road residing Herald car.......
Or was it just two Raleigh bicycles with child
seats at the back – one maroon, one emerald?
For the journey back to our village home
For that evening and next morning's task
of preparing yet more blackberry bathing

This time to convert the black sea crop into a special jam
One which the bees and wasps would squeeze through
every crack in the kitchen windows and doors
to try and sup yet more of nature's hallucinates
A few more scary hours avoiding painful stings from the
	angry charged insects
Before calm returns and sighs of tiredness
Drag us off to our peaceful sleeping chambers
For the long restful hours, days, weeks, months, year
Before we can wake again and swim in the dark blackberry
water heaven of the River Itchen and Stonebridge land
Special country haven of my Grandma,
my Mother and their Mother's Mothers

NATURE'S NURTURER TEACHER

My mother had another past
Too buried in her sad country to want
To create new growth, new nature
................................but she did have me!!
Father was different
Farming and labouring was his blood
Growing and feeding were his life's tasks
"Show me, feel me, nurture me"
He heard, he was given and so he gave

Why was it his natural instinct?
Why did he seem to be showing its love to me?
(just like they taught me love)
It was something without words
He never spoke about his emotions
Unlike her, reflection alone enabled
its presence to be seen

Repeating actions, time filled duties
Man's passion talk is always kept silent
Except for anger – that can be shouted and shown

But placing tiny, innocent, free grains of
seemingly nothing into nature's mother earth
and nurturing their place to transform them into
incredulous life
Things that feed us, amaze us, rivet us
Giving us our surroundings, painting our backgrounds
Created by us or enabled by us to be created?

Do men want children from the same root?
Our human language echo's that of green nature
Seeds, roots, grains, sprouts, blossoms, fruit
Children follow the same spoken words
But their nature – how is that nurtured and taught?

Dreams of garden tendering men
Waiting for their seeds, roots and sprouts to
blossom and fruit
Upright un-expressives,
Un-observing of all but their fields and tenderer tools

I approach like them but very unlike them
They turn me on, they excite me, they fear me
My nature is what they offer
Not nurtured nor taught
Growing, foraging, being like men
But punishment is coming
The fellows prepare to inject me with pain not nature
But that I have recorded in another place

Dreams of feeding
Dreams of growing
Father's instincts inserted into
my seed root, ending my nature?

So, all that is left is unspoken
Repeated actions, time filled duties
Seeking, foraging, preparing, feeding

LYING ON THE BACK LAWN

The summer that boiled us
Was 110 at No.59 in '76
But just like many lingering summer days
With no beach for a hundred miles
I rushed out the back daily
To that enticing green lawn

For too many hours
Towel down, swimmers on
Laying almost naked, still and flat
And ready to receive the free rays
Grabbed by one innocent youth
Chameleon or bliss or dreams?

The Chameleon
Desperate now to make myself someone else
Tanning that youth-less, ageless skin
A new colour ritual
But it involved inevitable fear
From one hour to many
Scorched red and burnt
How fresh was my skin now?
Two days of pain and a lifetime of fear from
Ten minutes of a fantasised new look
With whom, for whom?

The Bliss
No one else but me
Surrounded by nourished gardens all empty
No sounds save the ecstatic birds
Singing out the pleasures of their children, well fed, well fled
All the warm insects would now be theirs
Lying arms outstretched, legs straight

Skin touching and feeling soothed by the texture of the lawn beach towel
The wonder of sun burning caresses
In my great horizontal easiness
Gentle trance-like breaths come and go
As I rest balanced on the edge of consciousness

The Dream
Falling over that crest into slumber
Pleasant thoughts, images, dreams fill the gap
My melancholic soul
How long will I live, how young can you die?
What if I were you and you were me?
Beautiful cousin's body, sibling-less love
Exciting home, endlessly welcomed attractions
Shorter reflection on his place in mine
Back to being in his skin, feeling his mind, seeing through his eyes
Ah! That fantastical reality momentarily touched

But did I ever see your faces watching us, resting above us?
In my dreams long time ago in another world
After them, after you, after me
Smiling and beckoning me with tears of loss
As you know the future and await my presence

But oh! my innocence
No chameleon, no false me please
Bliss and dreams, that is the real me.............
Bring back sun-filled June
On my family's grassy back beach

DART IN THE HEAD

What a disastrous time
The day my world nearly ended
And it predicted the same for our country

My brother and me, young teenage seekers
Always seen as two, together bound
Never knowing ourselves
Lazy Sunday afternoon between two choirs
"Let's fill our time with a battle" we shout

Into the dirty dark world of working shiny tools
Up on the wall with the circle to compete on
Drunken pub game for old men
The choice in itself showed our unfound identities
Loosely fingered flying stabber
Thrown to pierce the highest quadrant
Maths to show the victor

I had lost
"So, go and pick them up David!
and I will go on practising,
throwing up and over you, into the board"
But then loud shrieks from him and me
I have lost my twin self, I thought
Stabbing him through the head
He fell to the ground

Then did someone utter?
"45 years you will be given, if he lives, to remain with us"
They were right, society's weapon has now struck back
Stabbed in the heart and head
Our choice that day showed the country was doomed
Dart in the head
Brexit had then been fed
To live for all those years until now
Paying us back for my thoughtless act

RAT IN THE BIKE SHED

Is nature evil, to whom?

Every morning I stepped into the wooden home
Of my beautiful mauve Raleigh bike
"Look at its elegance, it's raciness,
taking me foot and step onwards every day "

One autumn dawn undoing the lock
I carelessly dropped the keys
As I stooped to the ground to retrieve
The corner of my little left eye
Caught an unexpected sparkle and I froze

Could my special cycle see me now?
A torch left shining all night?

The light turned off and I jerked with shock
Through the door's crack I observed it
I gently, nervously, held the handle
And slowly opened the woodshed door

For a short second the darkness held
Then as shocked as me, it ran past so fast
It's frighteningly large brown long-tailed speeding image scared me then
As it does today, as I sit here and write

One actually small, barely understood creature
My head full of pre-learned false fear
Led to weeks of torture and teenage distress
My bike, its bedroom, now sullied
My daily morning wake-up, now too scared
Why did this innocent creature cause me pain?

Natural animal, unnatural evil
Created by man
Unnatural human, natural evil
Created by all mankind

AND SO, I SAIL AWAY FOR ANOTHER DAY

And so, I sail away for another day
Gliding foot on pedal up and over
Teenage first or last journey to my own school
Journey created to stamp my identity
And a love of balanced and ever turning wheels

They gave me those feelings
My parents affirmed by gemini children
Their boys gleefully seated each behind their forward motioner
Empty country lanes passed through
En route to their and our special motherer

They gifted me a royal Raleigh
"Too tall for you at first, but take it now
and build your motion love on wooden blocks
filling the void between toe and pedal"
Then show them success
Through transferred strength and controlled power
And golden cycling proficiency

Back to weekly morning
First following parent's motherly path
Then their working route
Onto the rest alone

Down the royal hill and fly over the canal
To the tricky oft' flooded rail tunnel
Victorian library never visited
And old folk's homes, many too many
Past the park where racket sports began
To finish with that inward heave to upward reach
And final sail down to school hall yard
Where fellows and boys, who's strength I had reached

Oh, the dismay my parents were to feel
When their joyful launching of my bike
Led me off to take away their dreams

CHANGING BEDROOMS

My first conscious defining moment as me
Choosing to be on my own
Leaving my womb brother's dream room
Here's how it came to be

I have no memory of my place in David's room
Just a hidden certainty of its truth
Like all those things from long before
That you only heard about from others
And which now became your past
But this recall is truly mine
   firmly in its original space

Mother came so urgent to inquire
Nothing neutral in her look
One question, so keenly searching for an answer
"Do I want a place just for me?"
How could I understand its meaning,.
Me versus me and him, what did that imply?
To sit, rest, sleep, wake, work...............alone
Solitary and separately
My things just for me
My decisions, my life from now on
My own window, my own outlook
How could a content, happy, lucky boy say no

The day passed and my hope was filled with excitement
But it was soon
to be slammed with a brutal reality

Same mother, same look, came by again
quick to tell, as before, sure of her mind
"if you leave David's room"
(already defined, no longer mine)

"we will never let you go back!"……
CRASH……………
The walls have fallen, the floor collapsed
Falling to sit astride my new existence
Me, not me and him
It was our shared womb, but only my placenta
Only can I rely on me, from now on

15 years of liberating solitude followed
Until my choices led to my second David
And then 15 years later, when she had departed
Father returned me to my brother's room
For 20 more years of re-feeling

Now he has gone, the room is gone
No bedrooms to move to or back from
I can reflect …….
Eventual gratitude for her helping me to take that first step alone…

CLOSE BY OUR NEIGHBOURS FENCE

Peggy and Andy
Sheila and Harold

Close to or just close by
Those names echo through the years
Faces familiar....
    But so is the dawn
        and the dusk

Divided just, but always, by a
short uneven fence
And a silent visible wall that
All our lives we lived beside

As children we were allowed through
for games and gossip
with their children
And returning we traversed the line
Bringing curious intimacies of their reality
For our adults to frown and never understand

Not once did we all share a table
Or a drink
Or even an hour's time in one place
Save to witness the tolling of the bells
As time travelled onward to
The etching out, one by one,
of the letters of their names and soon of their images

But a long felt nearness
Translated to warmth yet
empty of discourse
Gave definition and strength
To that boundary and its affection

Sheila and Harold
Peggy and Andy

CHASING MY FATHER

I was certain then:
Their love, like the love they gave me, was faultless;
She ruled the roost, and he agreed, always;
I never had fear, for him or her;
Until that moment

In a quiet room, or was it just sound-full but secure?
Broken by the sudden, jagged, awakening smash of the front door
I rushed to the window, knowing yet un-knowing
He walked away, measuredly fast,
The back of his head revealing his anger

Chaos broke my soul at that instant
As I rushed out,
Terror drove me on to resolve
Emptiness, loneliness, an eternity of his loss

My anxious temper drove my legs on
Racing to catch his wind rush air,
I caught him halfway round the block and
grasping his hand – a beggar's sob
I looked at that face for some small offering

No, this, my principal man
Was not leaving but rather revealing
A walk to exhale his bad air
And then to inhale back a calmer softness

So, now nothing was certain – least of all everything
Never again would that be for me

Not then, but now I see
Love and dependence – both unseen and seen
Must both present themselves to allow
Togetherness to endure

DAD AND ME AT SKY BLUES

My sadness and the cool winter sun
Takes me back to our only time of shared togetherness
Those open-aired stadium blues of my teenage years

Was it both my parent's or his sturdiness?
Or natural twin competitiveness?
That drove my interest in sport
I hesitate to use the words passion or love
But maybe sport made me feel an OK male
And allowed me to follow my eyes for desire

Whatever: he and I, and the two others,
Sharon and her dad,
Bought and brought us to the nearest city's venue
Medieval Coventry, Highfield Road, Sky Blues
A home team spirit was found

Whether cold, wet or just a little too warm
We would park, walk, then file into that place
Standing and leaning, chanting and rattling
Scarf waving for a glorious victory

No, not at this mediocre, just about place,
But he and I and we all rejoiced
And together, we focussed on a collective spirit
Until my future choice drove me away north and I never came back

It wasn't bliss, not even close
Shared Saturdays or even week day evenings
of distraction and attachment,
devoted to diverting our un-entwined minds to
at least point in the same direction

Sad it was that it ended
Never to be re-kindled
Not even when surprise led that
middling team to reach for greatness,
National elation at the country's stadium,
But father just would not join me at that place,
For one never to have been forgotten day,
Waving those scarves and driving the
Sky Blues' boys on to sparkle and to victory

PART II

ABOVE MY PLACE

We have been in the sky all night
Racing to reach one home
Two hours rest

But I do not know how fast I could face
getting to be with him
Too slow or too swift, endless agony
His resting place awaits

Guided on a familiar route
Crowning the Chiltern downs
I gaze out in a sad daze as
Light tears weep from the misty grey sky

A dark red dot grows as it sweeps towards me
I see its mission
To swoop down and find my soul
"Pick me up, into the sobbing air", I say to the red kite,
"Take me on your back, to gently ride the skies of my home"

Halfway to heaven
Time reaches forward and back
As I hover and glide over
familiar lands and memorable faces
Ancestors and successors
Aged oaks that have lived and
will live through all our generations

Harmony now in my timeless flight
Alone, yet always with my
gracious winged beauty,
The generous crimson air-glider who
keeps my spirit from flooding with pain
As all it seeks is to touch
him with a calm peace at his end

LYING BESIDE THEM

Lying beside them

Fully clothed
Skin and bones
Sunken beauty
Swelled delight
No movement

Ah, an imagined breath

For ever that milli-metred space separating you
and me
Them and us
Life and not
After life and yes
Moments eternal
Now and whenever
it comes

WHAT IS MISSING LOST?

What is it, what is missing, what is lost?
Is it a foundation stone or a jigsaw piece of my life?

I awake and try to understand
The picture in my head is like a square or boundary
With a big hole or corner taken away
My skull has a deep dent

What can I do with the missing and lost?

I think I must walk around the edge, the wall
To assess the damage and fix it
But inside I know that this is going to be impossible

These precious life stones are never going to be re-acquired
I must just live what is left
Guarding my broken soul and making do till the
Death tsunami sweeps in and breeches the injured edge,
Crushing all the rest

What is missing is lost

IF THEY THINK THAT WILL HELP, THAT'S OK

They think it will help?
They will help
OK
That will help if they OK?
Will it think, that they OK?
K.O. will it?
If they help
Thow if it
What we know
Nothing OK

BEING INSIDE DYING FATHER'S AWAKE HEAD

Being inside a dying Father's awake head
Alert to hear
Alert to get frustrated
Floating, hallucinating, dreaming, reality, unreality
Words on the wall
Words about the wall

And then crying, crying, crying
Small tears, no sound

OUR ETERNAL DRINK

Not solid not liquid
Only downed together
In a cup, not in a cup
Only just felt on the tongue
Aromatic peach
Tasteless snow
As it soaks our bodies
We drift away

MOTHER, WHERE ARE YOU!!!

Between her legs I came
Between my legs I sit
Bewildered and lost

THE JOYFUL AND LOVING DESCENT OF FOOD

Inch by inch account
Physical and allegorical story of
Life's pleasures of food

My father's inner body
Home to a well roundedness
That would welcome, be courteous and then pass on
Always one to relish and enjoy a good meal
With his friends, family, or on his own
From his Royal Marine role as a supplier and warden of meat rations
To his production job in local vegetable gardens

A fork or spoon would be held up in joy
As it made its ascent to the mouth
Such anticipation, such oral delight
Liquid spinning thickly in the rising spoon
Held still to maintain its fullness
Yelping beans and squeaking meat
Eager to fall from their stabbing forks

Mouth waiting and wondering how the next morsel will make it feel
It's desire to make them swirl on his radiant, expectant tongue
A certain warmth will keep them there
The battle to conquer the largest pieces and turn them into
small lumps that can be swallowed swiftly down the throat

The soft moist slide into the acidic stomach
Rolling, smothering, maybe even caressing the
oozing oesophagus' ageless wall

What do they know of his living and dying body?
They only know their own death roll
As this man's killer liquid shrinks and pushes them on
But this is a loving descent and they smile grimacingly,
Onto the walls of intestinal slowness
As every perspiring drop is gradually sucked out
to feed his loud, angry organs

Crushed together they re-form as dark cloaked lards
Jolting, squeezing, inching, the ghosts move forward
These new forms seem to know their part
Taking as much time as possible they
wind down to the radiated jagged fragility
of his twenty-five-year-old wound of destiny
This will be the last time he or any of them
come to this soundly greeted, well-rounded figure

The final act of their passage is upon them
As I lean on my father's daily delirium
Hearing two words uttered soundly and three words madly
Closely ushering in our childhood dreams
I glance down as he cries frantic tears
To disbelievingly, joyfully, see that unblemished young man's belly
And below, my only ever glimpse of his manhood
Showing me the descent end's awful dark finale

The last jubilant journey of food through my father
Marks his final un-nourished body's woeful waning wail.............

MUSIC IS FOR ALL FOREVER

Idyllic untouchable unconscious
Utterly discernible connection
Love and warmth
In William's resting place

Boys and girls
New women and men
I will remember their example
"wishing you a blissful ecstatic Merry Christmas"

Sensory fullness
All around receiving in all the body and soul

Jazz means Christmas funk
Unpredictable rhythmic street disunity
Greatness heaven

Belfast musician and teacher
Something special

Shine a light, shine a light on every corner of our hearts

Which ones of you are like me?
Moving, shaking, mouthing, swinging to
touch my vibrating reach

Wide open shining eyes to transmit our
joyful tears into yours

Little rapper boy wrapping us up for Christmas together

The ones that have to hold their music
To their eyes to remember and emit
The ones that put it down to remember and sing loudly out to
Fill this sacred place with their passion
And translate it for us

I AM SEARCHING FOR YOU MOTHER

I am searching for you mother,
Please hear me, my father is looking for you
He wants to join you soon
So, he needs your presence now

I have been searching for you since you left
Or maybe since you left my love behind
Nearly forty years of absence
The pain has flooded and retreated
and flooded again,
My fears of your discarded love
have given me many traumas
Sometimes when the painful storms came
Sometimes during the dry season
But those daytime nightmares
have fuelled my pessimism

Why my love for your love could be allowed, by you, to seep away
into the drains of your street,
Just because of my chosen love,
I will never know

But if you tell us where you are,
We can rekindle our touch together,
Those original gentle caresses
From the affectionate feathers of my mother hen
and your gift to me
Returned to you by my fluffy body,
muzzling against your soul

Let us back in – we cry
Let us in

TEARS DEEPEN THE SOUL

Sudden sadness sinks deeper
The all-seeing eyes slouch shut
Opening to seep, enveloped with warm inner water
Tears trickle then flow fully
My body brushes the harsh sad wall
Tingling against the grey-aired reality

But as the inner eyes release their liquid again
My enriched feelings grow and grow
Vast expanding vistas of new thoughts
Fill the long seconds as they keep me so still
This is a new place, so rarely seen
My soul, this must be my soul

The tears which have filtered down,
fuelled by my father's last fleeting moments,
have begun to expand my life,
keeping these precious learnings coming
until the tears cease and the soul's tongue retreats

BLEAK BURTON DASSETT BLISS

As I ride abreast him, my red kite flies, gliding me above
Closer to the lanes and fields of my birth
I glimpse the small treeless grassy downs
Cut out of the valleys and villages
And a place which we loved so deeply

Would this Saturday be warm enough?
Would we be free of choir singing duties and weddings?
Would there be no family chores to do?
Would grandma not be free?

But maybe once a month from May to September
The navy Herald was woken up and in we would dive
Our ecstatic arousal was fed by a sky as blue and crystal clear as the sea
Maybe the sea's mesmerising allure was reflected
to our meridian land by the sun's silver reflecting glass?

This place was not blue but oh so verdant green
Grass kept low by our white fellow country livers
Since medieval times placed here to take the trees away
Their woollen beauty ruling our countryside

However it was made, its beauty was undeniable
Such steep slopes, ready-made for rolling games
It's old quarry, full of fossils and other curiosities
The rounded peaks, vistas unexplainable but injecting such elation

Children's legs full of limitless energy
Running on ahead knowing our family would follow so far behind
Then we glanced back, atop a grassy mound, to show our strength
"Who's the king of the castle?"
And they had gone – or at least we feared they had
So, do we charge back or keep on exploring?

Our contented family gave us the latter's confidence
Gently spiralling we went up to the stone tower
In other places, it would have had wooden wings
and spin in response to the wind
But this was no windmill, that had long gone from its nearby place
This golden Cotswold stone tower was erected
To tell all around of its restful location
Signalling it was there for all to see
Hundreds of square miles around
They would see this place, as we, that day, could look at them
As they waited for their "lucky" Saturday bliss
On this bleak, but always smiling out,
Warwickshire Burton Dassett refuge for all of life's ills

YOUNG AND OLD SKIN

Connected with ageing, it changes how it rests,
Protected from the air, that place never ages
It sits, connected above and below, to fellow cells
They have enjoyed and endured life's happenstances
But not this child-like unsurfaced surface

As I, perhaps too intensely, watch my father's final encounters
My fingers yearn to touch and caress,
and my eyes to ceaselessly rest
on this small peaceful piece of his body,
A few squirls of teenage hair on his soft flat belly,
Memories of a soft unblemished child,
Fill me with surprised joy

Please let that un-aged youthful segment of his skin
Tell me a wished for lie:
No sun, no bones, no death

But alas, as I dream away reality, I awake
This innocent piece of my "baby" father
Has its ageing poison only from within
He has no young, only beautiful deceiving charming old skin

MY BRAIN IS FLOATING IN A COLD PAINFUL LAKE

My brain is floating in a cold painful lake
Rubbing hourly against glaciers full of powerful senses
And being pushed along by cool breezes of rich feelings
The lake is full of green water plants and floating debris
of dead leaves and broken branches
Handing me infinite thoughts on anything and everything

I never imagined in my full, but obviously limited life,
That so many powerful imaginings could catch me

However, I almost feel like I am approaching
a time not rich and full,
But one of blankness and devoid of anything
I know and fear for when this time will come
Mine or his time, it will be here soon

And I ponder
What is worse?
The freezing liquid of the great painful reservoir
Or the calm warm emptiness?

25 DECEMBER 2018

Floating in an almost dead live world
And then at 3am on the 25th he floats off
And you have nothing to hold you up
So
      you
          sink.....

PART III

THE AGEING FACES OF THE WORLD

The ageing faces of the world
Walking towards me this sad Christmas morning
I look so intensely at every one of them
Their eyes, their movements, their engagement with each other,
And then to see if they look at me

Everyone passes me by
As a few minutes of their life passes by
My intolerable intransigence of sadness,
Their oh so bearable living gestures

But all of the thirty minutes of
my walk along the streets, beside the river of this town,
will be soon gone,
As this world's other agers will also be gone
This seemingly stationery moment of my loss
Cannot be still............

PASSING BY

They have now all gone by
As we walk along the river Avon's sun dappled path,
Shadows of tree's winter branches
are carefully stepped around
There are no eyes to look at or movements to catch
Only gold and black monochrome dazzles
Hands firmly in our warm pockets feel our own presence

Walking as far as the town's milestone
We cross the un-landscaped iron bridge over the weir
As we do so we are edging closer to his rest home's gate
The gate is unlocked but will not be opened by us today,
And I now realise the purpose of this morning's slow march

He is no longer there
Christmas rituals drove them to take him out of his death bed,
to a more sombre place full of fellow threshold passers
Where he rests peacefully awaiting my mother's arms,
On New Year's Eve I will go there
To share a few minutes of his resting

But for now, as we walk back to town,
I know that I will come back to the riverside room of his last days
To see his bed, connect with his soul and feel his dying presence

LOOKING AT HIM

Here I am
Here he is
In this quiet sun-filled back room
Are they horse carriages outside in the yard?
No, that's my own dream in this old family-run respectful place
Are those gardenias I can see filling this room?
with the fragrant scent of their wedding?
By who's miracle where they placed here?

I will sit over there and pray a little
Quietness and a wished for feeling of God's presence penetrates me deeply
Then moving towards him I feel his body's loss of its soul

So, I just want to stay here in a timeless stillness
And spend hours or whatever's left of my lifetime
Meticulously imagining, touching, watching and feeling
the me-ness of his skin and body
Understanding just a little in each second
of the minutiae of his love

HIS AND MY CRYING EYES IN UNISON

His and my crying eyes in unison
Are we sad – yes
Are we in love – yes
Will we always be together - yes

HE IS GONE

He is gone
I will be gone all too soon
What is time?
What is life?
What is living?
What is leaving?
20 years ago she left
20 years before that I left
Now I am back and he is gone
Sleeping in their house
Me and mine finally
Before time again starts counting
Till our departure

I AM TO BECOME A CHILD NO MORE

What made this race to the front of my tear-soaked mind?
An only just lightened and deepened soul
Felt its presence this evening
At Hansel and Gretel

Those familiar names from our early years
Transformed into an adult show
In an opera house of royalty

As the story progresses
Boy and girl, children together, like me and David
Playing innocently in familiar woodland scenes
Joyful memories of lively and free exploration
Juvenile, barely explained observations
Leading to unprepared for gravitas

Oh, those often dreamed-of characters
Enticing, then searing our simple minds:
Rapunzel, her long hair and her entrapment
Red Riding Hood and her witch
Cinderella's lost love
Sleeping Beauty and that kiss
Foxes dancing with all

Surrounding them all
Are a chorus of chants and a big band full of majestic chords
Filling the forest with much too many
melancholic Christmas-like hymns
Drowning the auditorium and my soul
with this winter's withered truth

Like the aged listeners to the nursery rhyme opera
Glimpsing back to their youth
My soul fills with doom
Of the end of all of my life's childhood being

No more bedside stories
No more parents in this world
I am to become a child no more

I LAID AS HER, NEXT TO YOU

I laid as her next to you
Please lay next to me both of you
As we always shared that bed
Make that emptiness never come
One, two, three nights
All time
Peace

MY HOUSE IS YOUR HOUSE – YES?

I am an utterly romantic soul
And these short yet seemingly long few weeks have reminded me
It's like my life of learning and yearning romantic-ness
Has been reaching out for its pinnacle and
now every tiny musical chord or simple word
entrenched deep in my love memory
pushes out instant tears from my bright eyes
To weep – yes
But to place me instantly, repeatedly onto that love pedestal

Lucia Popp your voice squeezes out the love tears like no one else
Arabella and Mandryka
Mein haus wird dein haus – sein

WHERE DID MY KNOWLEDGE AND INSTINCT OF LOVE COME FROM?

From the tingling sensation of their romantic passion?
To the entwined months together with David in her womb?
To the painful joy when they released me into light?
And the four of us enveloped together in bed every morning?
My early senses filled my heart and my learning spirit

So that connection with them and my
constant observation of their love
filled me with an innate desire to have my own
It enabled me to always be in the moment
to receive what was there now and rejoice

Even though they chose to close their displayed
love for me because I had become me,
I knew what the love was that I
felt, needed, gave and would never toss away
And so, when my David arrived in my life
I soon knew he would always replicate
and I would always return to him
My life's love's true essence...

PART IV

SEARCHING TOO LONG FOR HER,
I PONDER WHERE I AM

Long, long, way to go
Up and down
Far away over the seas
Where I once was and as I once became
But am I dreaming?
Am I drowning?
Fathoms deep

Look through the port comes the moon-shine astray
It tips the guard's cutlass and silvers this nook
I'm sleepy and the oozy weeds about me twist

I fear to bid farewell to you all
Never your joys no more
Farewell to this grand rough world
Never more shipmates, no more sea,
No looking down from the heights to the depths

But Ah, I have sighted a sail in the storm
The far shining sail that's signals her torch
I'm contented
I've seen where she's bound for
She has a land of her own where she'll anchor for ever
Don't matter now being lost, or being forgotten or caught in the weeds
I know where to go and I'll yonder seek

(Inspired by Jacques Imbrailo's performance of Billy Budd
BRITTEN, B. *Billy Budd*, ROYAL OPERA HOUSE, London 10 May 2019)

HOW DO SHEILA AND HAROLD'S ASHES INTERWEAVE

Hello my dear Harold
I've been waiting for you to come
I saw the boys bring you here a few weeks ago
I was thirsty for your breath
But it did not come

Today as the rising sun glistens
through the new leaves of this small woodland
My new age senses sparkle in anticipation

Twenty-three years ago, my youthful soul in its
too aged body came here and dropped its
infinite pieces into this earth
Then they regularly fed the spring effusing
emerald life you see growing here
But now they need a new life to re-charge them
which you will bring

Martin is now releasing you into my gently lined cross
David waits and prays as he gently cries
Twelve corners and four hands
Underneath, my new growth roots shake to
release your goodness from the fragile grey
and silver remnants of your old life on this living moon

And now the moisture in this our simple "Gethsemane"
Brings a freedom of movement
to our combined fragments as they entwine
Oozing delicious eternal kisses
Freely bringing our country land its future zest for life

WHEN A HUSBAND JOINS HIS WIFE

When a husband joins his wife
Their lost years can be left behind

No words can really tell
The infinite yearning
The paradisiacal hope
To be again with your life's chosen love
He dreams as she longingly entices him
And tingles as he feels those visions
But linger he must.........as he has done

His thoughts are of the lonely swan as he
Passes his glorious shining fellows, still entwined together,
Forlorn, but certain he must watch life
from his solitary place until his
winter coloured wanderer arrives to
sing his swansong and fly him
far away to rest above the clouds
His shimmering wings holding the sky's air
To float there with his mate

Nature's life reaches its end
And all must re-join to flow, as the mighty rivers do,
To let his sun give birth to the future followers
To begin from the smallest to the greatest

Hallelujah, Hallelujah to the clouds

THAT CAT'S FACE IS LIKE MY GRANDMOTHERS

We never had pets at home
Neither did my grandmother
Except the six chickens,
Well 21 chicks bought in a box for Easter
One by one they were slayed by Grandpa for dinner
Last two were Tom and Jerry
Jerry was last

When I created my own home with David
Cats were always there with us
All called Lucy – loved and nightly entwined
As close as close could be
It gave me a new pet cat connection
Not fully realised then

Until I wandered around our northern French village
A course through Courset
Regularly walked, nature absorbed
Birds calling lovers, hundreds of them filling the sky
with their familiar phrases

Then up walked a ginger tom, pretty and confident
Were they grey or blue eyes looking at me?
We stood close, but apart, in our examination
and assessment
Then he came to my side and gently meowed,
Letting me rub and caress him

As we continued those few minutes together
His face turned again
Those features were not just his, but hers
Was this my grandmother Doll?
For these moments I felt she truly was her
But maybe all our cats were her
Knowing my grandmother's greatest legacy:
Unwavering love
And all our cat's emotions:
to give Martin and David and their family feelings forever,
How could they embody anyone else

Now I will take my last Lucy's ashes and place her remains with Gran
They will be one incarnate

HOLDING YOU

Sitting here on my bed, holding my love's hand
I tingle with raw emotion longing to describe
every element that my father's skin brought to me

Skin, why skin?
It embodies our body and its aging
The surface of all beneath
The thing we use to feel others

Mother's joyful caress
Brother's angry playful punch
Lover's enticing touch
But my father
        –   Then I thought of nothing

His hands, wrinkled yet strong
Hard work, bent bones, angled off centre
Nails barely recognisable, rarely cut
These hands reached out
But often held back from a loving role,
My eyes examined as with all,
Connection of men, resting on a table or desk
The yearned for touch of a man's hand, but never his,
Until I saw his romantic days of sailor and dater
Those images aroused my nostalgic desire
Today they define his world weariness
These hands' last role is to be rattled into her ashen palms

What wrists have rested those hands
Tough connectors of touch to his life
Seemingly small, yet so strong
The softest skin, delicately wrapped around
As the rest weaken, these stay solid
Ready to part define him, even after he's gone

Wrist to arm to shoulder
Soft fleece to protect this man's muscle
Weapons for war, sharpened by this young soldier
To guard him in his shallowness
Revealed to all, this masculinity
Worn through life, worn by life
Fallen biceps, shrunken triceps
Still threatening, or so he says

Armour's breast? not on this one
Blond to grey, fur to warm
Or more likely sweat, as the body
Too earnestly kept his heart alert

To his unshown, unworn, unblemished panel
Between mother's connector and lover's penetrator
Was it her who kept this skin like a childs?
Even as death drew its scythe in the belly's hair,
Oh, warm my cheeks on this baby boy

His legs aged faster than all
Bones skewed, ending his travails
Stumbling along with new insertions
Operated and replaced
Still he could move forward - ever slower
But not on those stairs, which lost his glimpse
as he fell to the bell,
The legs caught him, twisted him
Saved him

Look at me now, your eyes are gone
A face that was closer to tears than smiles
Probably was always made that way
Save the midway decades
When your joy was aroused by her endless affirmation
But then too, weeping was close,
As you hid from us the pain of her weekly collapses
Always covered by an oath of lies

As you fell to bed, not death,
Your death crept back,
But gave me you,
For an intimate final togetherness act
Just a month, forty thousand minutes
to linger together, skin adjacence,
Seeing, touching, feeling

YOUTH'S TRANSFIGURATION

I have now started living my thirty years you lived before I came
Will they bring me more of your early life in my latter ones?

I could dream infinitely of the end and its transfiguration in my youth
Dreaming and singing of an old man's wining
Of his waning to the end and his walk to the sky
Music of life's joyous melancholy
Unfathomable, utterly unctuous

With chords in harmony, Strauss echoed my heart
I could do naught akin to him
Only walk my pen
That nib, its fantastical freedom to express in an unknown world

I felt the way he did at his end
"Dying is just as I composed it when I was twenty-five"
Have I thought and written, as him, truthfully?
Childhood's innocence
Struggle of manhood
Battling between life and death
Yearning and attaining the infinite reaches of heaven?

So, I will go deep into my imagination
to your start
and its trance will walk with me...

THE FORTUNATE MAN

Anxious, tired, exhausted he sits here
Bleary eyes trying again and again to focus
on something........ anything
Failing to see, to know what is in front of him
He keeps his mind open to examine the image
Of a ruby red but nearly dead ripe strawberry

Am I hungry? No that's not why I want it
My tongue craves for something soothing
Radiant taste, delicious fragrance, almost liquid feeling
This will ease for a moment, my drying, fading mouth's senses
I reach for the fruit's presence, my fingers shaking in anticipation

And then I drift back in time
With poignant echoes of someone's music
Am I Ashenbach or Tadzio? Longing or just watching as the minutes
    count by?
Those that stayed on this life island know they will die, why do we stay?
So again – what will that tender fruit bring?

What is my life's fortune?
I am at this place but I cannot help looking back
Many years have come and gone
Did I really look after myself?
I know I should have treated others better
Or at least as well as myself
I did not

You call me a fortunate man, but what is that?
Lucky to live, lucky to die?
Or just a blessed illusion for those I leave behind

You who will write their right and think that they will touch me

Keep going
I am waiting

FATHER'S GIFTED ISLE

As he rests upward and ever present in the arms of my mother
He sends this special gift to us as we sit in the sun and wrestle with
our life's pains

Day time:
My father cries: "Don't blink, don't let them blink!"
The sun eyes of the sky must always stare down
Placing blissful blue warmth on them
Here on their island of brief tranquillity
Sweetly breaking down their pain and grief as it sits with them
And helping its unbreakable threads thin and lengthen and spread out
wide over the ocean

Night time:
My father cries: "Don't blink, don't let them blink!"
The eyes of the night sky must stay shut
Darkness brings them restful sleep and blessed dreams of tranquillity
Here on my gifted isle
Only the shining kisses of the stars are allowed to break the pleasant
sleep-inducing blackness of these hours
The kisses will then skip along those now ocean-wide threads of grief
Enabling them to gently rise and fall on the waves and gain some
sweetness from the caresses of the night stars
And then begin the grief's transformation from all too long pain to
sweeter memory and reflected love

WHY DID GOD CREATE THE OCEAN?

To reflect heaven?
To allow us to drown our sorrows?
Or perhaps to give us a way of connecting to others

He knew man would take to floating
Like the birds he created would take to the air
Transport to fellows, fellows to transport
Connections that led inevitably to conflict of power
His creation knowingly created war
Soldiers transported across heaven's star reflector
Met and slaughtered

But for some lonely, empty men like my father
It gave them purpose, adventure, partnership
Loyalty and deflection from their parent's pain

But once learnt, never lost, as the sailor
found his way it could never be changed

No going back, no painful son love, only the
Floating solace of a solitary memory-rich mariner

THEY TAUGHT ME LOVE

I am so lucky
And so grateful for their gift.

5 December 2018,
"Where is my watch?" "What is the time?"
"Here take mine Dad".

Placed firmly but gently around his delicate wrist,
My watch became his watch,
Our shared time stood still,
For a precious while.

But then the seconds began walking again,
And mine and his time inched invisibly forward,
Moving towards our last goodbye.

Now that watch joins my wrist again,
As I hold my arm out to rest his arms in the
arms of my mother.

Sending my life's gratitude for your loving gift,
As you depart.

For ever,
With Sheila and God,
And your love.

(Read at Harold's funeral)

THREE DAYS OF SILENCE BY THE SEA

Three days of silence by the sea
We face across the ocean
Towards barely visible islands on the horizon
Lovers, children, friends, families, loners
Gathering on the beach in the scorching heat
We sit here above them
Fearing venturing to go down
The sea is just too warm

Now there is a blue sky that has come,
Yes, the sky's mood is also blue
A group of thin cloud islands appears above
Are there familiar people gathering on their beaches?
Then the clouds seem to dissolve into the blue sky
And it makes the sky turn a much darker hue
Has the water now turned colder?
Shall we now go down?

BEYOND ME THERE IS PEACE

Beyond me there is peace
Is it too far or just a moment away?
Morning awakens to birdsong and insects
As the sun warms, a gentle breeze returns
My path must take me through the day
Thoughts bringing both joy and angst
That wind must now blow hard before dusk will call it calm
Unknowingly blowing time along faster to tomorrow
Is that peace I saw, for today or for tomorrow?
Will the peace chime ever ring for today?

Lightning Source UK Ltd.
Milton Keynes UK
UKHW040736261119
354268UK00001BA/224/P